EUROPE'S
TOUGHEST
GOLF HOLES

TOM HEPBURN

SELWYN JACOBSON

Salem House Publishers
Topsfield, Massachusetts

Concept:
Tom Hepburn and Selwyn Jacobson
Text; Tom Hepburn

First published in the United States by
Salem House Publishers, 1988,
462 Boston Street, Topsfield,
Massachusetts, 01983.

© Copyright
1988 Tom Hepburn and Selwyn Jacobson

ISBN: 0 88162 326 1

*P.G.A. Health Warning

Golfing *can* affect your health. If you are thin-skinned, weak-kneed, lilly-livered or suffer from congenital high handicapping, the Publishers and Authors join with the P.G.A. in urging you, before venturing onto any of our illustrated holes, to visit your Professional. And, if you've any sense, your doctor, your ski-instructor and the Man from the Prudential.

If you do insist on aiming for the record books (*you qualify just by completing the 18 holes — any score gets a mention*) the following tips may assist you in correct club choice, keeping your score down and getting back alive.

**Posthumous Golfers Anonymous*

SOME USEFUL DEFINITIONS

The Uphill Lie

McBaffie, in his "*Not On The Level*" (93rd edit.) insists the legs be well spread and the club gripped an inch further down the shaft to guarantee accuracy.

Casual Water

Golfers scorn taking the penalty drop from water, when all that's needed is a little application and a firm grip.

The Elements

Inclement weather *never* means an abandoned match. Perhaps an extra sweater, certainly a flask of Laphroaig.

TRANSPORT & BASIC EQUIPMENT

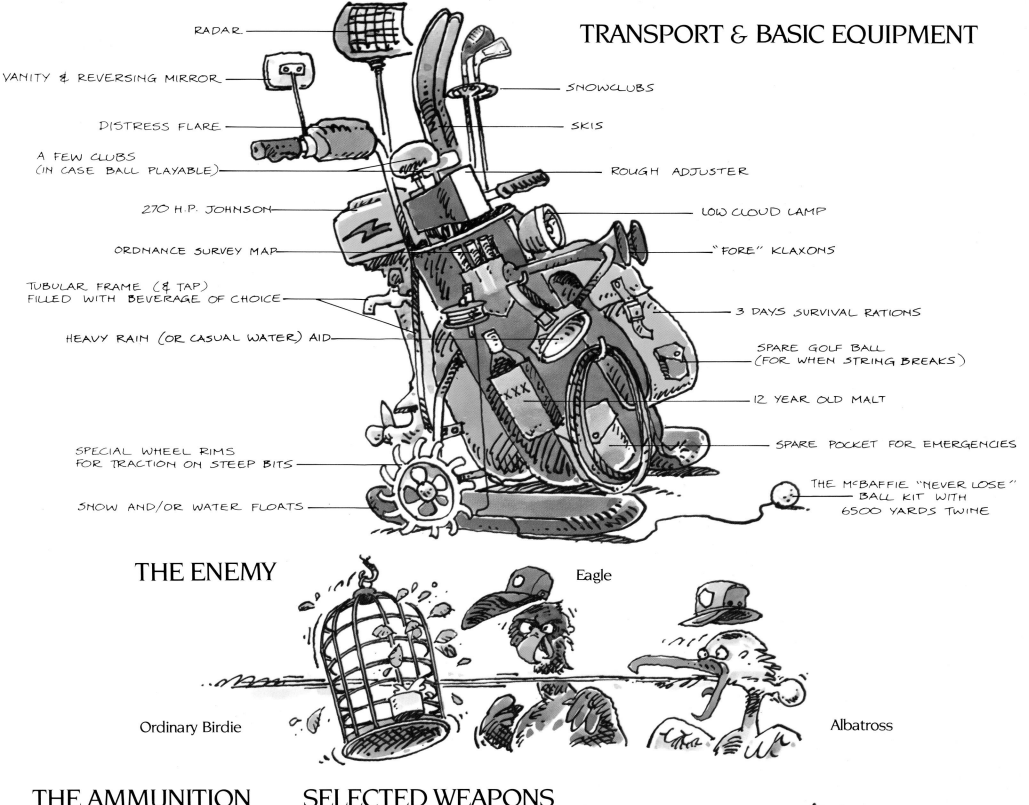

RADAR

VANITY & REVERSING MIRROR

DISTRESS FLARE

A FEW CLUBS
(IN CASE BALL PLAYABLE)

270 H.P. JOHNSON

ORDNANCE SURVEY MAP

TUBULAR FRAME (& TAP)
FILLED WITH BEVERAGE OF CHOICE

HEAVY RAIN (OR CASUAL WATER) AID

SPECIAL WHEEL RIMS
FOR TRACTION ON STEEP BITS

SNOW AND/OR WATER FLOATS

SNOWCLUBS

SKIS

ROUGH ADJUSTER

LOW CLOUD LAMP

"FORE" KLAXONS

3 DAYS SURVIVAL RATIONS

SPARE GOLF BALL
(FOR WHEN STRING BREAKS)

12 YEAR OLD MALT

SPARE POCKET FOR EMERGENCIES

THE McBAFFIE "NEVER LOSE"
BALL KIT WITH
6500 YARDS TWINE

THE ENEMY

Ordinary Birdie

Eagle

Albatross

THE AMMUNITION

Small British   Large American

SELECTED WEAPONS

1. Baffie: long approaches; sheltering behind during
   storms; emergency firewood supply.
2. Spoon: shallow (less than 1.8 fathoms) casual water;
   scoop shots from crevices; measuring Scotch
   into coffee.
3. Cleek: deep water recoveries — running noose catches
   ball, or with luck a fish.
4. Niblick: for taking divots on rocky surfaces; repelling
   wild animals; running amock with in mixed
   foursomes.

ROLLO'S REACHES
175m par 3 out + 220m par 4 in

As with so much of Normandy's lifestyle, golf course architecture owes a lot to the Norsemen who, some years ago, made their presence felt along this inhospitable coastline. Indeed, they are held solely responsible for altering beyond repair many of the rules and regulations set down by Charles Simple III, the then Senior Administrator of the G.P.G.A.*

This little seaside course has scarcely changed since those early, formative years and the two holes photographed - out to the 17th, back in to the 18th - are typical of the simple savagery so beloved of the men from the North.

Gaul Professional Golfers Association

B A L L E R O
395m par 3

THIS attractive if fairly straightfoward little course never lacks for excitement, and for a very interesting reason — the back nine are laid out inside a stud farm for bulls. Each Sunday golf takes on a new meaning for those brave enough to play a full round, and when you hear the comment on the 19th "I say did you see that amazing charge from the 15th?" you can be sure birdies had nothing to do with it. An intriguing local rule here states that 'any golfer striking a bull, with club or ball, shall lose the hole and his ears'. Fortunately this is offset a little by players being allowed to carry a muleta as a 15th club. And visitors, if they've any sense, will take advantage of the caddierilleros, who can advise not only on club choice, but where to stick them!

BLANC CZECH
650m par 6

THE deceptively large green here (1.3 hectares) tends to make even experienced players underclub on the approach, though once on the green it's just a question of settling down to some steady work with the putter. Other holes offer other hazards, however, and many the prominent visitor who has left his mark around the course. Rodriguez McCorkindale the Auchtermuchty Amateur, three fingers and a 2-wood up on the 8th, and De'ath Haute-Savoie 'the Berne Basher' both wheels from his new buggy and most of his nose after spending a night trapped in the big fairway bunker of the 15th, spring readily to mind.

But perhaps none so infamous as that fine golfer from Czechoslovakia, Nikolaus Wenceslaus. Niki was the only one from that terrible Christmas tournament in '07 not to make it back to the Clubhouse. Last seen heading resolutely into a snowstorm up the 5.5 km long ice field which forms the 12th, dressed in his usual flamboyant all-white gear, he was never seen again.

Today a pair of crossed baffies mark the spot where he was thought to have played his last fairway iron.

GENDARME
250m par 3

PLAYING with policemen
is one of the slightly unnatural hazards encountered
by golfers everywhere, but in provincial France
such an event takes on an extra *frisson* as 'la peur
du gendarme' often lasts well into adult life. This
fascinating hole, not unexpectedly known as 'the
gendarme' (from its uncanny resemblance to a
uniformed dummy directing traffic) was for this
reason the scene of considerable embarrass-
ment to a visiting foursome of English
clergymen. Losing their way, as men of
this vocation so often do, on the long 3rd,
the group finally stumbled on a small village
where they sensibly enquired at the local police
station where they might find the 4th hole. Alas,
their French was imperfect and the request "ou
est le trou du gendarme?"** resulted in their being
thrown into jail. They were released only when they
gave their names as Langer, Nicklaus, Ballasteros and
Jacklin — a little white lie which any God would forgive.

**translation on request

OLD HARRY'S ROCKS
210m par 3

THE love affair of Harry Penhaligon for Deirdre McBaffie — a torrid affaire which had gossips from Bognor Regis to the Bill of Portland at it for months (a bit like Harry and Deirdre, actually) — came to its sad end on Swanage Links. Deirdre, paired with none other than a certain Tom Morris, fell out of love and in again during the first 9. Harry, a Dorset man to his last long vowel sound, could not compete with the mellifluous tones of Tom's erotic brogue and had to watch, silently seething, as young Morris holed par followed by birdie followed by eagle . . . until Deirdre was all but swooning at his feet. Berserk with frustrated lust, Harry, mashie flailing, ran at the innocent Morris with murder in his eye, failed to see a loose impediment underfoot, tripped and plummeted into the broiling foam. Young Tom, almost (though not quite) looking up from a long putt, was heard to mutter "Puir auld Harry's aff his rocks" before sinking another birdie.

DOG LEG
660m par 5

ONE
of the
more tedious
problems facing
course architects working
on new layouts above the 3000m
line is making allowance for future ava-
lanches. This potentially round-spoiling occur-
ance is most excellently illustrated here on the
Eiger's 'North Face Nine' as locals affectionately call
it. For years the difficult 7th, photographed, would remain
unplayable for most of every winter save to the hardiest of
golfers, until an elderly member, dragged in for the fourth
time during a single competition by the Club's St Bernard,
hit on the answer. Simplicity itself! Fit a tiny radio trans-
mitter to every ball and a receiver to the dog, and no
matter how far a ball was carried off course, the faithful
hound would seek it out and return it from whence it
was struck. Penalty stroke, of course, but at least
players could complete their rounds.

18TH GREEN AND CLUBHOUSE

THE dedication of the Dutch in their desire to excel in every field is exemplified in this tranquil winter scene. Hard to recognise in the fading light, but putting out on the 18th green, is none other than the legendary Erasmus van Hoek, known to his fellow members ever since he pulled his drive on the 1st into the Caddy Shed (stunning old Willem van der Valk in the process) as 'The Original Hook of Holland'.

Erasmus, like many another Frisian before him, was short of temper; yet he controlled his wrath, buckled down and became not only Club Champion but Convenor of the Social Committee too.

IL DOLOROSO
470m par 4

AS one might expect in Europe, many of the golf courses are redolent with history. Some indeed are red for another reason — blood! Yes, sad to say, Italian clubs *have* been raised in anger, and on occasion with good reason. Consider the intriguing case of Bonaparte (famous artilleryman) vs Finione (famous chef) and their grudge match here at D.D.C. Irritated beyond measure by Bonaparte's pompous pronouncements concerning elevation of green, striking force of clubhead, weight of ball, trajectory and wind speed, Finione buckled down and thrashed his employer 6 and 5. Enraged and humiliated, Bonaparte called up his favourite cannon *La Bearnaise* and proceeded to annihilate the course (and unfortunate players) hole by hole. Today evidence of his pique may still be seen in the fairways here at the 17th. Even the Clubhouse was destroyed, but members confidently expect it to be rebuilt soon. Work, as may be seen in our photograph, has already begun on the new Pro Shop.

SWAN SONG
185m par 3

IT is a constant source of relief to the German people, so often criticised for their meek acceptance of authority, inability to cope with lateral thinking, and general stodginess, to be able to point, with justifiable pride, at Ludwig Wittelsbach, creator of the least ordinary golf course in the world. Ludwig, who also doubled as King, was fed up with wars (he never could work out whether to support Austria or Prussia) and got together with brother Otto - whose approach to Full Quid status was never more than half way - and his mate Dick Wagner, a popular song writer. Between them they designed the fascinating 18-hole course at/in/over and through Ludwig's holiday home. It hasn't yet featured the German Open, but it certainly pulls in the tourists!

MUCKLE CHUCK
506m par 4

WE all, surely,
have engraved into our minds
the ineffable words of Jock
Nickerless, who wrote, in his
5-volume definitive work — **'Swingin'
In the Sixties — A Glaswegian's
Lament'***(Drumnadrochet Press, 16/4d)*
"Grip it tight, haud it stright, gie'd a dight — an'
keep yer ee aff the ba'!" This esoteric advice, neglected
by most, nevertheless paved the way to victory for the
legendary Porthos McBaffie (pictured), 7th son of the 7th
son of old J.B. himself, at the Auchterarder Open in '87 —
the youngster's first public appearance since the
unfortunate affair of the strangled caddy.
Perhaps it was the clean Highland air; perhaps
the sheer talent of the lad; more likely the
flask of Laphroaig which never left his bag:
but suffice to say the breaking of the
course record, the claiming of the
Hole-in-One prize, and, in the post-
victory euphoria which followed,
the unexpected defloration of
the Vicar's eldest, all made
for a very successful tournament!

SAILOR'S REST
120m par 5

O.K., so this course is just nine holes - but what would you expect on a 150 acre island swapped by the Brits for Zanzibar? Hospitality here is unique, however, and the course is particularly popular with passing trawlermen, who hold their own Stableford twice a week. Young ladies from the mainland make a point of being on hand in case caddies are required, or something! The Clubhouse (on the right, lee side of the sea wall) is small but with a saving grace - it never closes. Once inside, visitors will inevitably be told the story of how the British designed the entire course in one afternoon - they detonated the largest known non-atomic blast (1947) and, hey presto! There it was! Except, that is, for the 8th fairway, which suddenly wasn't. It does lend the course some distinction though - it is the shortest par 5 in the world.

PILATE ERROR
540m par 5

As a rule, golfing anecdotes in Swiss 19ths don't always make the blood race. Something in the national character seems to turn out golfers who seldom stray far from handicaps in the 8-15 area. But as though to prove the rule, visitors to this fine mountain club are invariably thrilled to hear the tale of old William 'four-eyes' Tell, at his very best never below a 36 handicap. Though powerful he had problems with alignment and couldn't putt for toffee. But even Will had hidden reserves. One day out on the practice fairway, he was duffing 9-irons quite happily, his son picking up balls for him, when out of the blue the youngster screamed in terror! Looking up quickly (and thereby hitting his first clean ball of the day) Will saw what seemed to be a ghostly figure above his son's head, dressed in a toga and continually washing his hands. Rightly guessing this to be the spirit of Pontius Pilate (whose body had been thrown into a nearby lake some years before) William whipped out his 1-wood, teed up three balls and blasted them clean through the wraith, not even scratching the boy! "One for the father, one for the son — and take that, you bloody ghost !" snarled William as he struck superb drives. After the 3rd ball the apparition dissappeared. A close shave indeed!

P I S A   P U E R

220m par 4

THE famous Sicilian professional and part-time tenor Arno Palermo not only designed this lovely course, but introduced into it what was then a revolution in teaching techniques. This elevated practice tee was built a short wedge high and a medium putt out of the perpendicular on Arno's specific instructions. He emphasised the psychological benefit to beginners of 'getting the ball in the air' quickly and thought this the best way to do it. Indeed, this scheme worked very well, until the sad day when young Luciano ('Lucky') Pisano (introduced to the game by his brother Nicky) leaned too far into a ball and swung himself over the edge after it. Arno was intrigued to note that both ball and and 'Lucky' fell to the ground at similar speeds, but before he could experiment further, the tee was banned to beginners, eventually becoming integrated into the course proper.

REEKIE WRECKER
460m par 4

ROYAL and Ancient does seem to sum it up rather well! When a king, no less, can be chastised publicly for 'the playing of the gowf' (and so imperiling the defence of the realm) then, boyo, you've got yourself a game to be taken seriously! In Edinburgh, as befits the place where it really did begin, certain citizens are privileged above others. They are life members of the most exclusive golf club in the world (eat your heart out, Pebble Beach) which is of course within the confines of the Castle. Membership is restricted to the Regiment-In-Occupation, members of their families with handicaps less than 24, and any Royal who happens to be passing and fancies a game. Play commences daily with the world's only Cannon Start, by Mons Meg at 1pm.

TANKS FOR THE MEMORY
105m par 3

THIS used to be an easy par 4, a
narrow but straight fairway leading to a pretty island
green. Until, that is, a group of Germans from Lubeck
(citizens from this city have had reciprocal playing
rights here since 1525) were
deemed by the foursome behind to be spending
a bit too much time looking for lost balls.
The irate quartet who took such exception to the slow
play were, as fate would have it, Afrika Korps officers on
leave, and as this was in 1943 they were able to back up
their argument with considerable force. Alas, the
approach to the green was changed forever -
yet, was it really all for the worst?
Bornholm gained a superlatively tricky par 3, and the
Germans lost the war.

FURROWS
580m par 5

As
mountainous countries go, Holland is,
perhaps, flatter than most - but this does not mean
its golf courses are any the less difficult. It is an
old golfing maxim that if there are insufficient
natural hazards - create a few! Here to
compensate for the inevitable 'up and down'
nature of the course, the Greens Committee
have devised such delights as ploughed
fairways, continuous water hazards,
and floating 'bunker barges'. And,
during the growing season a penalty
stroke must be taken for every
tulip beheaded, by
clubhead <u>or</u> ball.

VIEW FROM 9TH TEE BACK TO THE CLUBHOUSE

PERHAPS because of the gradual 'coming of age' of golf in Europe, strange and intriguing finds, which have perplexed archaegolfogists for years, are now becoming headline news. Only recently, in a special Romansh edition of the *Lenzerheide & Filisur Eagle Fanciers and Mountain Goat Breeders Gazette*, the front page carried the following item. It seems that a threesome, sheltering from an unseasonable avalanche in the Members Only cave by the 17th, were moodily practising chip shots when one accidentally unearthed what has since been verified as an Ostrogothian Cleek (circa 493).

Alas, an unseemly scuffle over ownership saw the club broken in three - but does it lend weight to Swiss claims that **they** invented golf ...?

H E A D S   I   W I N
880m par 4

BACK in the good
old days, when Valhalla still had rooms to let, golf was the
only real man's game available. Your average Viking,
after a hard campaign of conquest, pillage and
rape, needed some outlet for his high spirits. Not
surprisingly he turned to golf, and most famous
among such men is surely the legendary
Snede Samsson. You'll remember at once the
Pro's Edda describing how he'd take the Fat Cats
of the Fjords? Pro for many years at this very Club, Snede
as a youngster would challenge any Viking to a sudden
death playoff at this hole, the mark to use a full set of
clubs and Samsson to play with but a putter and his
favourite two-handed twin-bladed driving axe.
After getting a good laugh at his opponent's
inevitably short drive, Snede would swing
his driver, lop off the head of the unfortunate Viking and without grounding his
axe belt the head clear across the
water and onto the green — often
to putt out in 3. Yes, one of
the great golfers
of all time!